YORKSHIRE

AN ILLUSTRATED YEARBOOK

1994

YORKSHIRE

AN ILLUSTRATED YEARBOOK
1994

Illustrations & Text · Simon Bull

Appletree Press

First published by The Appletree Press Ltd, 19-21
Alfred Street, Belfast BT2 8DL. Illustrations ©
Simon Bull, 1993. Text © Simon Bull, 1993.
Printed in the EC. All rights reserved. No part of
this publication may be reproduced or transmitted
in any form or by any means, electronic or
mechanical, photocopying, recording or in any
information or retrieval system, without prior
permission in writing from the publishers.

Front cover: Pen-Y-Ghent
Back cover: Emmerdale Farm Cottage

ISBN 0 86281 417 0

List of Illustrations

Contributor

Simon Bull

Simon Bull is one of Yorkshire's most outstanding and successful young artists. Born in 1958, he graduated from Leeds Polytechnic with an Honours degree in Fine Art; since then he has developed an international reputation for his watercolours and etchings. He prefers to work from direct observation, as his notes to some of his paintings in this Yearbook testify, and his locations range from Yorkshire to the Mediterranean and as far afield as the North-West Frontier of Pakistan. Simon Bull has carried out numerous commissions for large companies and is a member of the Yorkshire Watercolourists' Society. In 1989 he opened his own gallery in Bradford. He is married with two children.

He says of his own work: ''A successful watercolour is the outworking of a concentrated moment of creativity and requires the artist to harness all his creative and technical abilities in one brief but intensive outpouring.'' A strong religious sense underlies Simon Bull's work, and his delight in the wider creation shows through in his responsiveness to his subject, whether it is a fast-food restaurant in suburbia or the rugged moorlands of his native county.

Introduction

The original Yorkshire – the Yorkshire of the four Ridings – is a county of incredible contrasts and richness. Stretching as it does almost across the nation, it stops only ten miles short of Morecambe Bay on the west and runs north-south between the Don, Humber and Tees. The county's diversity lies partly in its size, but also in its geologically distinct areas that have literally become the bedrock upon which the economy and architecture of the region have developed.

In the north-western corner, the serene limestone landscape of the Dales comes to an abrupt end at Giggleswick scar, where the winding A65 holds it back Canute-like from the millstone grit landscape of the West Riding. Gradually the hills and valleys fall away to the rich farmland and water meadows of the Vale of York and the Wolds. Here honey-coloured or brick dwellings with red pantile roofs nestle among ploughed fields and woods. Farther south lies the triangular wedge of the South Riding, where coal and heavy industry have shaped the landscape. In the north-east the Yorkshire moors, with their bracing combination of heady, heather-scented air and long views, lead inevitably to the coast, where the shimmering waters of the North Sea draw the eye and imagination towards the infinite.

In common with all places where man has lived and worked for centuries, the landscape of the county has a story to tell. Added to the stories recalled by castles, abbeys and old mills are the unique impressions and memories each one of us has: memories that epitomise not just a place but an experience. Yorkshire the experience! How can it be summed up? Queuing up on Thursday at dinner-time for fish and chips wrapped in the *Telegraph* and *Argus*; the rancid odour of lanolin from the mills, mingling with the winter drizzle; high tea in Harrogate; scampi in Scarborough or on Ilkley Moor with or without a hat.

Inevitably our fondest and most nostalgic memories are securely protected by the passage of time, but like the seasons our world changes. We remember when the trains called at Ripon, or before the motorways unrolled themselves hungrily across the hills. With the passage of time not all traces of our journey are obliterated. Beneath the tarmac road surface the cobbles that once rang to the sound of clogs and horses lie dormant. On the wind-swept moor, stone pathways, polished by the feet of our ancestors, speak to us across the years.

It has been these glimpses of the old amongst the new that have captivated me in the production of this book. Take, for example, the Devil's Arrows at

Boroughbridge. The day I visited, the stones stood in a field of barley, overhung with mature sycamores. To the west traffic roared past on the A1; on the lane nearby, children walked home from school, their fluorescent coloured satchels adorned with the latest movie slogans. A hundred and fifty years ago the sycamores would have been saplings. The children are perhaps not so different. But go back further, perhaps to the time when the Romans were busy building the nearby settlement of Isubrigantum, now Aldborough. How does the landscape look now? The field patterns built as a result of the Enclosures Act are not present; has a forest grown up to hide the giant monoliths which even in Roman times were gnarled and lichen-covered with age? Who were those ancient tribespeople who toiled so hard to drag them into position?

In more recent times, our forefathers toiled in a similar way to construct monuments that have either passed into disuse or hang by a thread to their original purpose. The three-mile long Standedge tunnel, for example, cut out of solid Pennine rock, once the world's longest canal tunnel, has lain in disuse since 1944. The Ribblehead viaduct and Bleamoor tunnel, crowning achievements of the age of steam, now carry only light traffic. Since 1981, however, East Yorkshire (Humberside) has continued the tradition of engineering excellence with the completion of the world's longest single-span suspension bridge.

I am an artist who believes in working from life wherever possible, and most of the pictures in this book were done on the spot. This is for two important reasons. Painting outside with the wind attempting to remove your work from the drawing board does make photographic accuracy more difficult, but it increases the authenticity and creative content. The lines might not be straight, there might be splashes in the sky or midges in the paint; but the finished piece comes across with an immediacy more difficult to achieve in the studio. Secondly, I love the outdoors; to head out across the moors looking for subjects, with the skylarks rising into the blue and all around the solitude, is heaven for me. Alone with God, a flask of tea and a bag of paints. Soon, though, the shadows lengthen and the spell breaks. I must away, other voices call.

Simon Bull

YORKSHIRE

AN ILLUSTRATED YEARBOOK

1994

SIMON BULL

**CAPTAIN COOK
SCHOOLROOM
MUSEUM
Great Ayton**

The small town of Great Ayton is renowned for two schools, the Quaker boarding school and the little village schoolroom, now a museum, where the famous Captain Cook received his early education. This quaint pantiled building is picturesquely situated on the town's High Street close to the banks of the River Leven. It is open to the public regularly throughout the summer months.

Monday • Week 1

27

Tuesday

28

Wednesday

29

Thursday

30

Friday

31

Saturday
New Year's Day

1

Sunday

2

Monday • Week 2

3

Tuesday

4

Wednesday

5

Thursday

6

Friday

7

Saturday

8

Sunday

9

**BARNS NEAR
WEST STONESDALE**

Just west of Keld as the lonely B6270 begins to make its way to Kirkby Stephen across Birkdale common, there is a turning off to the north over Park Bridge. Swinging the car around a double bend lifts you up above the valley floor and towards the village of West Stonesdale. Four wild upland miles later and you arrive at the Tan Hill Inn. The route takes you past the remains of old mine workings and some lovely old barns linked by a farmer's track. It is a popular and much photographed scene, but even so, how could I resist such an opportunity to paint, with pockets of snow clinging to the gullies high above on Black Moor, and the soft light of earliest spring giving contrast and animation to the barn's ancient stonework.

Monday • Week 3   **10**

Tuesday   **11**

Wednesday   **12**

Thursday   **13**

Friday   **14**

Saturday   **15**

Sunday   **16**

ARNCLIFFE VILLAGE

The grey limestone buildings of Arncliffe are grouped around the rectangular village green with its ancient pump standing proudly in the centre. The Falcon Inn and village post office also face onto the green along with some interesting old barns; one fine specimen complete with porch has a date-stone of 1677.

Monday • Week 4

17

Tuesday

18

Wednesday

19

Thursday

20

Friday

21

Saturday

22

Sunday

23

SHOOTING BUTTS
Blubberhouses Moor

When I arrived on the open tops above Blubberhouses, the purple-brown heather was crusted with freezing fog; curtains of mist moved silently about me as I made my way towards the old shooting butts dimly silhouetted against the blackening ridge. Could this be real? Was I actually going to attempt to paint in this weather? Finding a cosy hollow amongst the heather I started work. It wasn't long before hot tea was being poured from the faithful flask, and surrounded by the cries of grouse I continued for several hours, as content and happy as could be.

SIMON BULL

Monday • Week 5

24

Tuesday

25

Wednesday

26

Thursday

27

YORKSHIRE SCULPTURE PARK

This magnificent bronze head by the European sculptor Igor Mitoraj is a fine example of the international work on show at the Yorkshire Sculpture Park. Set in the grounds of Bretton Hall just south of Wakefield, the park, which was founded in 1977, draws visitors from all over the world and is one of the county's major art attractions. There is a permanent collection of sculpture, as well as a regular programme of exhibitions and educational projects.

Friday

28

Saturday

29

Sunday

30

Monday • Week 6

31

Tuesday

1

Wednesday

2

Thursday

3

Friday

4

Saturday

5

Sunday

6

SID'S CAFÉ
Holmfirth

Brontë country, Herriot country, Cook country, and now Summer Wine country. The Pennine town of Holmfirth has found a whole new *raison d'être* as a result of the popular TV series "Last of the Summer Wine". Sid's Café in Victoria Square is one of the authentic Summer Wine haunts where tourists can partake of afternoon tea in the same surroundings as do Compo, Clegg and Foggy, three of the programme's most famous characters.

SIMON BULL

Monday • Week 7   **7**

Tuesday   **8**

Wednesday   **9**

Thursday   **10**

Friday   **11**

Saturday   **12**

Sunday   **13**

THWAITE

When Norse settlers arrived in upper Swaledale sometime in the tenth century, it is possible that some settlement already existed at the place where the village of Thwaite now lies. Either way it was the Norse who gave the village its name, which means "a clearing in the forest". All trace of the forest has long since disappeared, but the grey cluster of houses, which huddle beneath the patchwork of Kisdon Hill, invokes a timeless quality with their thick walls and lichen-covered stone roofs. When I painted this view, it was a windless March day of dense, slow-moving cloud. Overhead a vast flock of red-wings circled in preparation for the long flight north, while curlews, drawn by the season's tidal pull, announced their new arrival from the coast with shrill, haunting cries.

Monday • Week 8 **14**

Tuesday **15**

Wednesday **16**

Thursday **17**

HOLBECK
Leeds

Friday **18**

It is something of a mercy
that this little island of
industrial history has
survived the developers
and is still very much lived
and worked in. Large
numbers of these typical
red-brick back-to-back
houses were cleared to
make way for miserable
tower blocks and
motorways. Having no
gardens, the washing is
still strung decoratively
across the streets from
house to house, adding
sparkle and colour to an
otherwise harsh
environment.

Saturday **19**

Sunday **20**

Monday • Week 9

21

Tuesday

22

Wednesday

23

Thursday

24

Friday

25

Saturday

26

Sunday

27

HARTLINGTON POST BOX

Driving south from Burnsall to Appletreewick the road passes through the hamlet of Hartlington. Here in this tiny settlement are a number of interesting buildings and features: an old mill, a bridge over the stream, Hartlington Hall – a mansion now converted into apartments – and this old stone water trough. The trough itself bears an inscription long since obscured by mosses. When the afternoon sun falls on its green sides and the vermilion letterbox is reflected in the rippled waters, the trough emanates a simple beauty, for the most part unnoticed.

SIMON BULL

Monday • Week 10

28

Tuesday

1

Wednesday

2

Thursday

3

Friday

4

Saturday

5

Sunday

6

**McDONALD'S
DRIVE-THRU
Rotherham**

Rising like a phoenix from the ashes of the River Don's ageing industrial complexes, the neon sign of McDonald's Drive-Thru restaurant pierces the night air. Serving the needs of hungry commuters and shoppers at the nearby out-of-town supermarket, the ultra-efficient Drive-Thru brings a whole new meaning to the concept of fast food.

Monday • Week 11

7

___

Tuesday

8

___

Wednesday

9

___

Thursday

10

___

BARNS AT ARNCLIFFE
Littondale

''Don't cast a clout till
May is out'' is ancient
wisdom and impressed
upon me a new meaning
the day I painted this
view. I had been to this
exact spot earlier in the
year; on that occasion it
had been winter, but the
air was mild, enabling me
to work with no
discomfort. Now,
however, as the leaves
and blossoms of early
summer made their
luxuriant debut, the north-
east wind cut into me like
a knife. I persevered,
returning stiff but
triumphant to the car.

Friday

11

___

Saturday

12

___

Sunday

13

Monday • Week 12

14

Tuesday

15

Wednesday

16

Thursday

17

Friday

18

HEWENDEN VIADUCT

Saturday

19

Hewenden viaduct just
west of Bradford on the
road to Haworth is a good
example of the many
relics from the age of
steam that can be found
in abundance in the
Bradford area. Its
seventeen fine arches
curve gracefully above the
valley, with the reservoir
behind forming an
attractive backdrop.

Sunday

20

SIMON BULL

Monday • Week 13

21

Tuesday

22

Wednesday

23

Thursday

24

CONISBOROUGH CASTLE

Unlike its North Yorkshire counterparts in their rarefied settings, Conisborough Castle finds itself standing somewhat incongruously amidst the industrial suburbs of the Don Valley. Built circa 1180 by Hamelin Plantagenet, half brother of Henry II, the magnificent limestone keep has survived in almost pristine condition for more than 800 years. The castle is now in the care of the Department of the Environment and is open to the public throughout the year.

Friday

25

Saturday

26

Sunday

27

SIMON.BULL

Monday • Week 14

28

Tuesday

29

Wednesday

30

STANDEDGE TUNNEL

Built between 1749 and 1811, the Standedge tunnel is England's longest and highest canal tunnel. Probably the greatest engineering achievement of its time, Standege's three miles of tunnelling through Pennine rock stands proudly alongside other Yorkshire engineering monuments, such as the Ribblehead viaduct and the Bleamoor tunnel. In the absence of a towpath, barges were propelled through the tunnel by ''legging'', which meant that the men had to lie on their backs and shunt the barge along by pushing against the wall. The record for the fastest leg through the tunnel was made by David Whithead in 1914, who managed the extraordinary feat in one hour and twenty-five minutes. The tunnel was closed in 1944.

Thursday

31

Friday
Good Friday
Bank holiday

1

Saturday

2

Sunday
Easter Sunday

3

Monday • Week 15   **4**
Easter Monday
Bank & public holiday

Tuesday   **5**

Wednesday   **6**

Thursday   **7**

Friday   **8**

Saturday   **9**

Sunday   **10**

PARCEVALL HALL

Occupying a sheltered south-facing site near Appletreewick in Wharfedale, Parcevall Hall and its gardens are the legacy of one man's wealth, genius and devotion. Originally a fifteenth-century farmhouse, the dilapidated hall was bought in the 1920s by the architect and devout Anglican Sir William Millner. Sir William transformed the bleak site into a place of exceptional beauty with the help of a large local workforce. The grounds, which are now open to the public, were designed to make the best of the "borrowed" landscape, with the terrace opening out onto fine views of the surrounding fells. On his death in 1964, Sir William bequeathed the property to the trusteeship of the Walsingham Trust who now lease it to the Diocese of Bradford as a retreat and conference centre.

Monday • Week 16

11

Tuesday

12

Wednesday

13

Thursday

14

Friday

15

**INGLEBOROUGH
From Crina Bottom**

The ascent of
Ingleborough from Ingleton
takes the walker along a
rutted green road flanked
on either side by white
limestone walls, speckled
with bright yellow lichens
and moss. Eventually the
hill comes into view, the
old buildings at Crina
Bottom providing an
admirable foreground. One
of the famous three
peaks, Ingleborough rises
to a height of 723 metres.

Saturday

16

Sunday

17

Monday • Week 17

18

Tuesday

19

Wednesday

20

Thursday

21

Friday

22

PEN-Y-GHENT

Windswept, bleak and often brooding, the distinctive whale-back form of Pen-Y-Ghent crowns the ridge between Horton in Ribblesdale and the road from Stainforth to Littondale in the north. Reaching a height of 694 metres, it is ascended along the Pennine Way, which leads the walker up the stepped southerly face onto the flat summit, from where one of England's finest views opens out on a clear day.

Saturday

23

Sunday

24

Monday • Week 18

25

Tuesday

26

Wednesday

27

Thursday

28

WHERNSIDE

Friday

29

At 736 metres above sea level, Whernside is the highest though least spectacular of Yorkshire's famous three peaks. Standing guard over the Ribblehead viaduct, it carries the Settle-to-Carlisle railway across Batty Moss. Completed in 1875, the viaduct is one of the wonders of Victorian engineering achievement. One of the central arches soars 105 feet above the ground – not bad when you think that the Humber Bridge is only 150 feet above the Humber.

Saturday

30

Sunday

1

SIMON BULL

Monday • Week 19
Bank holiday

2

Tuesday

3

Wednesday

4

Thursday

5

Friday

6

Saturday

7

Sunday

8

THE BRIDGE HOUSE
Whitby

There have been three drawbridges of differing types on the site of the present Swing Bridge which straddles Whitby's fascinating harbour. The first was built in 1766 at a cost of £3,000; the second in 1835 cost considerably more at £10,000 but was somewhat larger, having a central span of forty-five feet and three inches. The present red-and-white swing bridge is electrically operated with a span of seventy feet. It is controlled from the diminutive bridge house on the western side.

Monday • Week 20

9

Tuesday

10

Wednesday

11

Thursday

12

Friday

13

COTTAGE WINDOW
Appletreewick

Appletreewick must be
one of the loveliest village
names in the Dales. The
village itself is also one of
the prettiest, its stone
houses draped with
climbing plants, lining the
steep main street between
Low Hall at the foot of the
hill and High Hall at the
top. The shadows of
Embsy Moor across the
river provide a fitting
backdrop to this sleepy
rural idyll.

Saturday

14

Sunday

15

SIMON BULL

1994　　　　　　　　　　　　　　**MAY**

Monday • Week 21

16

Tuesday

17

Wednesday

18

Thursday

19

Friday

20

**ALMSHOUSE AT
LEATHLEY
Near Otley**

A weathered plaque,
unreadable in places,
declares for posterity the
philanthropic generosity of
Henry and Ann Hitch who
erected and endowed this
''school and hospital'' in
the year 1769. Over 200
years later the almshouses
at Leathley are still
functioning as such, and
the Ann Hitch Trust,
although eroded by
inflation, still continues its
charitable work.

Saturday

21

Sunday

22

The Olde Sweet Shop

AGENT FOR
BENTLEY
CLEANERS · LAUNDERERS

SIMON BULL

Monday • Week 22

23

Tuesday

24

Wednesday

25

Thursday

26

**THE OLDE SWEET
SHOP
Pateley Bridge**

Originally believed to have
been the servants'
quarters for the town's
apothecary, the Olde
Sweet Shop was built in
the early seventeenth
century. Apparently
haunted by a lady in blue,
it is now much more likely
to be haunted by hungry
tourists eager to stock up
on Yorkshire Full Cream
Fudge and the like. The
shop's humble appearance
certainly adds character to
the steep main street, and
I confess to having
indulged in a box of fudge
myself – but strictly for
''research'' purposes!

Friday

27

Saturday

28

Sunday

29

SIMON BULL

Monday • Week 23
Bank holiday

30

Tuesday

31

Wednesday

1

Thursday

2

THE RED LION
Burnsall

It is summer. In the trees chaffinches fill the air with song; the peat-stained river murmurs under the bright noonday light. The cries of children at play blend with the passing traffic. This is Wharfedale in summer; yes, this is Burnsall – far enough away from Bradford and Leeds to be out in the Dales, but close enough to make it home comfortably on time at the end of the day. With its village green fronting the river, tea rooms and that most Yorkshire of all pubs the Red Lion, it is small wonder that this picturesque village is such a popular destination for many a day trip.

Friday

3

Saturday

4

Sunday

5

SIMON BULL

1994   **JUNE**

Monday • Week 24   **6**

Tuesday   **7**

Wednesday   **8**

Thursday   **9**

FOUNTAINS ABBEY

Founded by the
Cistercians in the year
1132, Fountains Abbey
was dissolved and
plundered by Henry VIII
after 400 years of
prosperity and influence. It
is now Europe's largest
monastic ruin and attracts   Friday   **10**
tourists from all corners of
the earth to its dramatic
setting in the River Skell's
narrow wooded valley.
The grounds are invitingly
laid out with a network of
broad pathways, and the
ruins themselves provide   Saturday   **11**
endless opportunities for
children to play hide-and-
seek, or for adults to
admire their aesthetic and
historical significance.

                                  Sunday   **12**

SIMON BULL

Monday • Week 25

13

Tuesday

14

Wednesday

15

Thursday

16

THE WHITE HORSE OF KILBURN

The slow crawl up Sutton Bank in my friend's father's ageing Saab, as we made our pilgrimage to the famous White Horse of Kilburn on my eighth birthday, is still etched in my mind. I remember too the feeling of being dwarfed by the 228-foot-high landmark whilst clambering over its whitewashed boulders. Ever since that day, whenever I have been out in the eastern Dales or in the vale of York, my eyes have always strained to catch that familiar speck of white which marks the beginning of the North Yorkshire moors.

Friday

17

Saturday

18

Sunday

19

1994

JUNE

Monday • Week 26

20

Tuesday

21

EMMERDALE FARM COTTAGE

"Excuse me, but do you know the way to Emmerdale Farm?" The question came from the window of a shiny limousine that had drawn up next to where I was painting. "Sorry", I said rather unhelpfully, but compensated for my ignorance by asking polite questions. Their answers revealed that the couple in the car had travelled all the way from Somerset in search of the elusive farm. After their departure I began to notice more vehicles creeping along with the occupants craning their necks at something – but at what? My curiosity aroused, I boldly popped the question to a pair of rambler-club types who stopped to admire the progress of the painting. "Yes", they beamed, "Emmerdale Farm is that building over there", pointing out a cluster of farm buildings behind me. Suitably educated I returned to my work, but as for Emmerdale Farm I am content to leave it "somewhere in Yorkshire"!

Wednesday

22

Thursday

23

Friday

24

Saturday

25

Sunday

26

SIMON BULL

Monday • Week 27

27

Tuesday

28

Wednesday

29

Thursday

30

THE EASTERN GATE
Studley Royal

Many are the times that
my school friends and I
would pass through this
arch together on Sunday
afternoons. It was a
modest walk to Studley
Royal from the forbidding
buildings of the Cathedral
Choir School where I and
my indomitable comrades
were ''billeted'' as
boarders. The archway
opened up to us a world
of adventure among the
ancient oaks, searching for
cast antlers in the deer
park, selecting choice
sticks on which to whittle,
and filling our growing
lungs with the
incomparable Yorkshire
air.

Friday

1

Saturday

2

Sunday

3

1994 **JULY**

Monday • Week 28 **4**

Tuesday **5**

Wednesday **6**

Thursday **7**

Friday **8**

Saturday **9**

Sunday **10**

LINTON TELEPHONE AND POST BOX

Enjoy this lovely old telephone box while you can: it will no doubt be replaced by an open-plan stainless steel or smoked-glass booth. Yes, they are a beast to maintain – all that paintwork, and vandals breaking the small panes of glass, but even so, with the removal of each one to the breaker's yard, our country loses yet another little spark of colour and charm.

1994　　　　　　　　　　　　　**JULY**

Monday • Week 29　　　　　　　　**11**

Tuesday　　　　　　　　　　　　**12**

Wednesday　　　　　　　　　　**13**

Thursday　　　　　　　　　　　**14**

Friday　　　　　　　　　　　　**15**

Saturday　　　　　　　　　　　**16**

Sunday　　　　　　　　　　　　**17**

AUSTWICK BECK

Rising high among the limestone outcrops of Ingleborough's eastern flank, Austwick Beck skirts the quiet village on its way to meet the River Wenning, which in turn swells the waters of the Lune just south of Kirkby Lonsdale. The village itself lies just off the busy A65, originally named by Norse settlers as Eastern Settlement. There is a market cross in the centre of the village testifying to busier times long since gone.

Monday • Week 30

18

Tuesday

19

Wednesday

20

Thursday

21

Friday

22

Saturday

23

Sunday

24

**FLAX FIELDS
NEAR YORK**

The low-lying farmland of
the Vale of York makes a
dramatic change from the
wild hill country in which
so much of Yorkshire's
character is expressed. It
is this very contrast which
makes the county so rich,
and a diversity of people
and places are seen from
millstone grit to
magnesian limestone, flat
caps to fish and chips.

1994　　　　　　　　　　　　　　**JULY**

25

Tuesday

26

Wednesday

27

Thursday

28

THE WHITE GARDEN
Newby Hall

Friday

29

Driving out of Ripon on
the Boroughbridge Road, a
right-hand turning takes
you on a pleasant tour
through the gentle
landscape of the Ure
valley, and after a couple
of miles the road reaches
the delightful Queen Anne
mansion of Newby Hall.
With an interior enriched
by Robert Adam and a
dramatic garden that
sweeps down to the
banks of the river, Newby
Hall and its gardens make
an ideal choice for a
family day out.

Saturday

30

Sunday

31

Monday • Week 32

1

Tuesday

2

Wednesday

3

Thursday

4

Friday

5

Saturday

6

Sunday

7

THE GARDENS
Ripley Castle

Half hidden behind a tangle of purple sage and regalia lilies, the iron gateway into the walled gardens of Ripley Castle stands invitingly ajar. Open daily from April to October, the gardens are also home to two nationally important collections: the National Hyacinth Collection and the Tropical Plant Collection, which was formerly part of the Botanical Gardens at Cottingham, Hull.

1994

AUGUST

Monday • Week 33

8

Tuesday

9

Wednesday

10

Thursday

11

OLD ROAD SIGN
Near Fewston

I hope no one from the Department of Transport finds this little gem and attempts to replace it with a more utilitarian and modern equivalent! One of the beauties of so many of our rural backwaters is that they are often overlooked by the more destructive tendencies of ''progress''. Adjacent to Fewston Church, this sign directs travellers in the middle of what was once a thriving community until much of the valley was drowned to make way for today's extensive reservoir.

Friday

12

Saturday

13

Sunday

14

Monday • Week 34

15

Tuesday

16

Wednesday

17

THE DEVIL'S ARROWS
Boroughbridge

Whatever their actual origins, the local legend about the Devil's Arrows and how they came about certainly makes a good story. Almost parallel to the A1 near Boroughbridge, the three stones stand about twenty-feet high in a straight line, two of them in one field and the other across a little road. The Devil reputedly hurled them at the village of Aldeborough, from the top of How Hill near Ripon. Happily enough for the inhabitants, though, his aim was not good and they fell short, leaving Aldeborough intact. Interestingly, Aldeborough is one of the few places in England with a continuous record of human habitation dating long before Roman occupation, when it was an important centre of Brigantia.

Thursday

18

Friday

19

Saturday

20

Sunday

21

SIMON BULL

Monday • Week 35

22

Tuesday

23

Wednesday

24

Thursday

25

HARRY RAMSDEN'S

No book about Yorkshire would be complete without a mention of its most famous fish and chip shop. ''I'm just wild about Harry (Ramsden's)'' goes the slogan, and who can deny the popularity of the restaurant which has a continuous queue outside whatever the weather, whatever the time of year! Those who eat at Harry's are not just buying reputedly the best fish and chips, they are also buying into the whole Yorkshire experience, an experience which is now being exported, with branches in Glasgow and as far away as Hong Kong.

Friday

26

Saturday

27

Sunday

28

Monday • Week 36
Bank holiday

29

Tuesday

30

Wednesday

31

Thursday

1

HAWORTH
Main Street

Friday

2

Since the decline of the woollen and textile related industries, much of the West Riding has passed into the realms of ''Industrial Heritage'', spawning a new and less gritty industry: tourism. The village of Haworth, with its nostalgic blend of rugged moorland, steep ''Hovis''-style cobbled streets and most of all the famous Brontës and their parsonage home, has become one of West Yorkshire's finest tourist achievements.

Saturday

3

Sunday

4

Monday • Week 37

5

Tuesday

6

Wednesday

7

Thursday

8

COTTAGE WINDOW AT RIPLEY

Owned for the most part by the Ingilby family, the present-day model village of Ripley was built in 1827 by Sir William Amcotts Ingilby, who based his original design on the villages typically found in Alsace-Lorraine. Each cottage is adorned with window boxes which are maintained by the castle's head gardener. Thanks to its ownership by the Ingilby family it has retained its unique character and has been spared the excesses of DIY enthusiasts and other home ''improvement'' schemes.

Friday

9

Saturday

10

Sunday

11

Monday • Week 38

12

Tuesday

13

Wednesday

14

Thursday

15

THE TOWN HALL
Ripon

Friday

16

In the year 866 Alfred the Great granted the cathedral city of Ripon its Charter of Incorporation. Since then the official hornblower has set the watch at 9.00 pm every night, by blowing the horn once at each corner of the market square and outside the house of the current mayor. The town hall proclaims in its maroon and gilt inscription the town's motto taken from psalm 127, verse 1: a word that for Ripon would appear to have stood the test of time.

Saturday

17

Sunday

18

1994　　　　　　　　**SEPTEMBER**

Monday • Week 39

19

Tuesday

20

Wednesday

21

Thursday

22

WILD ROSES

Whilst driving through the county's back roads researching material for this book, I was struck by the abundance of wild roses adorning the verges, not just because they were beautiful but because of their significance as the age-old badge of Yorkshire. It is five centuries ago now since the houses of York and Lancaster clashed in the Wars of the Roses, which ended in 1485 when the Lancastrian Henry Tudor defeated Richard III at Bosworth Field and became Henry VII.

Friday

23

Saturday

24

Sunday

25

Monday • Week 40

26

Tuesday

27

Wednesday

28

Thursday

29

Friday

30

Saturday

1

Sunday

2

RICHMOND CASTLE

Dominated by its impressive Norman castle, the market town of Richmond stands guard over the entrance to Swaledale. Building work began on the castle soon after the Battle of Hastings when William the Conqueror gave tracts of northern England to Alan Rufus as a reward for his services. Despite its strategic position the castle has never been attacked. It is now in the care of English Heritage.

Monday • Week 41

3

Tuesday

4

Wednesday

5

Thursday

6

Friday

7

Saturday

8

Sunday

9

RUNSWICK BAY

Most of the little coastal villages along Yorkshire's northern coast are so closely huddled along the cliff sides that they remain hidden from view until the last minute. The tiny cluster of houses at Runswick Bay is perhaps the best example of this. After a day foraging for subjects on the heather uplands, I drove to the coast following signs to the village. At first there seemed to be nothing there, just a row of semis and a pub, but then a further sign beckoned. Following the signpost's instructions I guided the car down a 1:4 gradient; as the road turned the corner the full beauty of the bay opened up before me. The tide was sweeping in with heady white breakers gleaming in the late afternoon sun. Away to the south, blue and turquoise beach huts shone like jewels against the shadowy headland of Kettleness. I made this swift sketch of the former coastguard's house before retreating from the spray of the rising tide which threatened to make its own special contribution to my creative efforts.

SIMON BULL

Monday • Week 42

10

Tuesday

11

Wednesday

12

Thursday

13

Friday

14

Saturday

15

Sunday

16

ANCIENT PATHWAYS

One of the most interesting and unique features of the North Yorkshire moors are the ancient paved ways, or Trods. The origins of many are lost in pre-history. It is possible that some were built by the Romans whose roads still cross the area, although most were probably laid down during the Middle Ages at the time when the great abbeys dominated the social scene. Certainly they were vital to the region's wool-based economy, enabling large caravans of pack-horses to transport wool down into Whitby or York. Today, however, with many of the paths cleared and restored by the park authority, the walker is presented with a wonderful opportunity to enjoy the countryside and to ponder about the lives of the men and women whose feet have combined to erode the gentle grooves and hollows in each stone.

Monday • Week 43

17

Tuesday

18

Wednesday

19

Thursday

20

Friday

21

Saturday

22

Sunday

23

LANDSCAPE NEAR OTLEY

I painted this landscape on a damp afternoon in early autumn; the lane is one of a network of scenic back roads among the hills north of Otley. In the background, the eastern ridge of Otley's famous Chevin rises towards the town, which is hidden out of view to the right of the picture.

Monday • Week 44

24

Tuesday

25

Wednesday

26

**EMLEY MOOR
TV MAST**

Crowning the broad east-west-lying ridge south of Wakefield, the Emley Moor mast has the distinction of being Yorkshire's highest man-made structure. The 392-metre-high mast dwarfs the ancient village of the same name that nestles at its foot. Now chiefly a dormitory village occupied by commuters employed in surrounding towns, the village of Emley was granted a royal charter in 1253 enabling it to hold a weekly market and five-day annual fair in May. The remnants of these traditions are still re-enacted during the Emley feast each May when the market cross receives its annual coat of whitewash and older residents put on special teas.

Thursday

27

Friday

28

Saturday

29

Sunday

30

Monday • Week 45

31

Tuesday

1

Wednesday

2

Thursday

3

Friday

4

**WAKEFIELD
Ancient and Modern**

The distorted façade of the cathedral is mirrored in the geometric panels of British Home Stores. This is an image that in its way reflects the character of Wakefield in the 1990s, with its brash and glitsy Ridings Centre shopping mall giving the city a new lease of life. Meanwhile the city's often disregarded but fascinating architectural heritage bears silent witness to the values of a former day and generation.

Saturday

5

Sunday

6

Monday • Week 46   **7**

Tuesday   **8**

Wednesday   **9**

Thursday   **10**

Friday   **11**

Saturday   **12**

Sunday   **13**

ASKRIGG
Wensleydale

The weather on the day I visited Askrigg was so bitingly cold, with the wind at such a force, that I was forced to transfer my equipment to the car and finish from the cramped comfort of the passenger's seat. This view, the most popular, shows the village grouped around the main street and sheltering at the foot of Askrigg common. The skyline is dominated by Addlebrough Hill, which is one of Wensleydale's most famous landmarks.

SIMON BULL

Monday • Week 47

14

Tuesday

15

Wednesday

16

Thursday

17

DANBY BEACON
North Yorkshire Moors

Friday

18

A centuries-old landmark
and vital communications
link for the nation in times
of peril, the gaunt post of
Danby beacon stands high
on the moorland above the
Esk valley. On the morning
I painted this, smoke from
burning heather rose in
dense billows from the
north. The constant music
of the wind as it played
out its low symphony
among the heather
rendered all other sounds
inaudible, save for the
staccato calls of red
grouse engrossed in their
annual courtship rituals.

Saturday

19

Sunday

20

SIMON BULL

Monday • Week 48

21

Tuesday

22

Wednesday

23

Thursday

24

Friday

25

Saturday

26

Sunday

27

MADONNA AND CHILD
York Minster

Presiding over the nave from above the western door the gilt statue serves as a reminder to the Minster's medieval origins under Rome. Thanks to careful planning controls, the Minster, northern Europe's largest Gothic cathedral, still retains its impressive dominance over the town's intricate network of narrow streets and alleys, many of which were laid down onto patterns begun in Viking times.

Monday • Week 49

28

Tuesday

29

Wednesday

30

Thursday

1

Friday

2

Saturday

3

Sunday

4

STAITHES

There can be few places that convey the romance of the sea as convincingly as Staithes. On the afternoon I visited, an old salt in a weathered blue smock tied up his coble in the sheltered waters of Roxby Beck. He returned my "Hail fellow, well met" greeting with a reluctant grunt before disappearing into the darkening streets. It was at Staithes that the young Captain James Cook had his first taste of the sea when he came to work in the village as an apprentice grocer in the early eighteenth century. The sense of the past is very real here, the large number of chapels conjuring up images of a once thriving community. On the tea shop walls sepia photographs of past inhabitants gaze down as the "land lubber" visitors sup their earl grey and listen to Vivaldi.

Monday • Week 50   **5**

Tuesday   **6**

Wednesday   **7**

Thursday   **8**

Friday   **9**

Saturday   **10**

Sunday   **11**

THE EAST GATE
Duncombe Park

Remarkably, Duncombe Park has been in the hands of the Duncombe family since its creation in 1713. It became a girls' school after the second Earl of Feversham was killed in the First World War, until 1985 when the present Lord and Lady Feversham restored it to a family home. The house and grounds are open to the public at regular times during the summer months.

SIMON BULL

1994   **DECEMBER**

Monday • Week 51

12

Tuesday

13

Wednesday

14

Thursday

15

BOOTHAM BAR
York

Friday

16

The bar, the belfry and the
bike: three enduring
symbols that represent
centuries of history on the
grand scale in this,
England's second city –
and Yorkshire's first.
Bootham Bar, one of four
bars or medieval gates
through the impressive
city walls, is seen here.
Resting against the
ancient mellow limestone,
the humble bike speaks of
man's transience in the
face of history, a reminder
that Vikings and Romans
once trod along the
streets of this great city.

Saturday

17

Sunday

18

Monday • Week 52

19

Tuesday

20

Wednesday

21

Thursday

22

Friday

23

Saturday
Christmas Eve

24

Sunday
Christmas Day

25

ARNCLIFFE CHURCH

Built on the northern edge of the village by the banks of the River Skirfare, St Oswald's Church has been restored and modernised with little of the original architecture surviving. However, it is still an impressive and beautiful parish church with a dramatic approach from the village. Inside hangs a list of the men from the village who lost their lives fighting the Scots at the Battle of Flodden in 1513.

Monday • Week 53

26

Boxing Day
Bank & public holiday

Tuesday

27

Bank & public holiday

Wednesday

28

Thursday

29

Friday

30

Saturday

31

Sunday

1

New Year's Day

TAN HILL INN

You know you have made it to the end when you arrive at the Tan Hill Inn – the end of the Dales and yes, of Yorkshire as well. North from here the valleys of the Tees and Eden fall away to the east and west, with the North Pennines of Cumbria and Durham dominating the skyline. At 1,732 feet above sea level, this is England's highest inn and one of the most remote. Tan Hill's electricity is produced by a diesel generator, the telephone is beamed in miraculously thanks to British Telecom's microwave link, and the heating comes from cosy coal fires, although bottled gas central heating is also available. For all its forbidding austerity, one can imagine the relief felt by weary, mud-bound walkers on the Pennine Way as the pub comes into sight over the endless expanses of peat and heather.